D1611361

Fun and Simple State Crafts

Fun and Simple Midwestern State Crafts

North Dakota, South Dakota, Nebraska, Iowa, Missouri, and Kansas

June Ponte

Enslow Elementary
an imprint of
Enslow Publishers, Inc.
40 Industrial Road
Box 398
Berkeley Heights, NJ 07922
USA

http://www.enslow.com

This book meets the National Council for the Social Studies standards.

Enslow Elementary, an imprint of Enslow Publishers, Inc.

Enslow Elementary® is a registered trademark of Enslow Publishers, Inc.

Library of Congress Cataloging-in-Publication Data

Ponte, June.
    Fun and simple Midwestern state crafts : North Dakota, South Dakota, Nebraska, Iowa,
      Missouri, and Kansas / June Ponte.
         p. cm. — (Fun and simple state crafts)
    Includes bibliographical references and index.
    Summary: "Provides facts and craft ideas for each of the states that make up the Midwestern
      region of the United States"—Provided by publisher.
    ISBN-13: 978-0-7660-2984-2
    ISBN-10: 0-7660-2984-0
    1. Handicraft—Middle West—Juvenile literature. I. Title.
    TT23.4.P65 2008
    745.5—dc22
                           2008018389

Printed in the United States of America

10 9 8 7 6 5 4 3 2 1

To Our Readers: We have done our best to make sure all Internet Addresses in this book were active and appropriate when we went to press. However, the author and the publisher have no control over and assume no liability for the material available on those Internet sites or on other Web sites they may link to. Any comments or suggestions can be sent by e-mail to comments@enslow.com or to the address on the back cover.

Every effort has been made to locate all copyright holders of material used in this book. If any errors or omissions have occurred, corrections will be made in future editions of this book.

♻ Enslow Publishers, Inc., is committed to printing our books on recycled paper. The paper in every book contains 10% to 30% post-consumer waste (PCW). The cover board on the outside of each book contains 100% PCW. Our goal is to do our part to help young people and the environment too!

Illustration Credits: Crafts prepared by June Ponte; Photography by Nicole diMella/Enslow Publishers, Inc.; © 1999 Artville, LLC., pp. 6–7; © 2007 Jupiterimages, all clipart and pp. 9 (all), 15 (flower), 21 (fossil), 27 (all), 33 (animal), 39 (all); © 2001 Robesus, Inc., all state flags; Shutterstock, pp. 15 (bird), 21 (insect), 33 (flower).

Cover Illustration: Crafts prepared by June Ponte; Photography by Nicole diMella/Enslow Publishers, Inc.; © 1999 Artville, LLC., map; © Jupiterimages, state buttons.

CONTENTS

WELCOME TO THE MIDWESTERN REGION!

North Dakota, South Dakota, Nebraska, Iowa, Missouri, and Kansas are the six states in the midwestern region. This area is referred to as the Midwest, because the states are located in the midwestern region of the United States. The geography of the midwestern states varies from

grasslands and prairies, to rocky lands and forests. Missouri's eastern border is formed by the Mississippi River. The state is mostly plains and prairie land. Nebraska is covered by plains, and most of the land is devoted to farming. The largest area of sand dunes in North America is in central Nebraska. Sand dunes are made of fine sand shaped into hills by wind. North Dakota

shares a border with Canada. Wheat crops grow well in this state's cool climate. South Dakota is home to many American Indians, including the Dakota, Lakota, and Nakota Sioux Nation tribes. The state has a prairie region and an area of badlands with unusual rock formations and deep canyons. Iowa has large areas of prairie land. The state is bordered by the Missouri River to the west and the Mississippi River to the east. Kansas has large areas of plains. Many of these plains are covered with fields of wheat and sunflowers. About 90 percent of Kansas is still farmland.

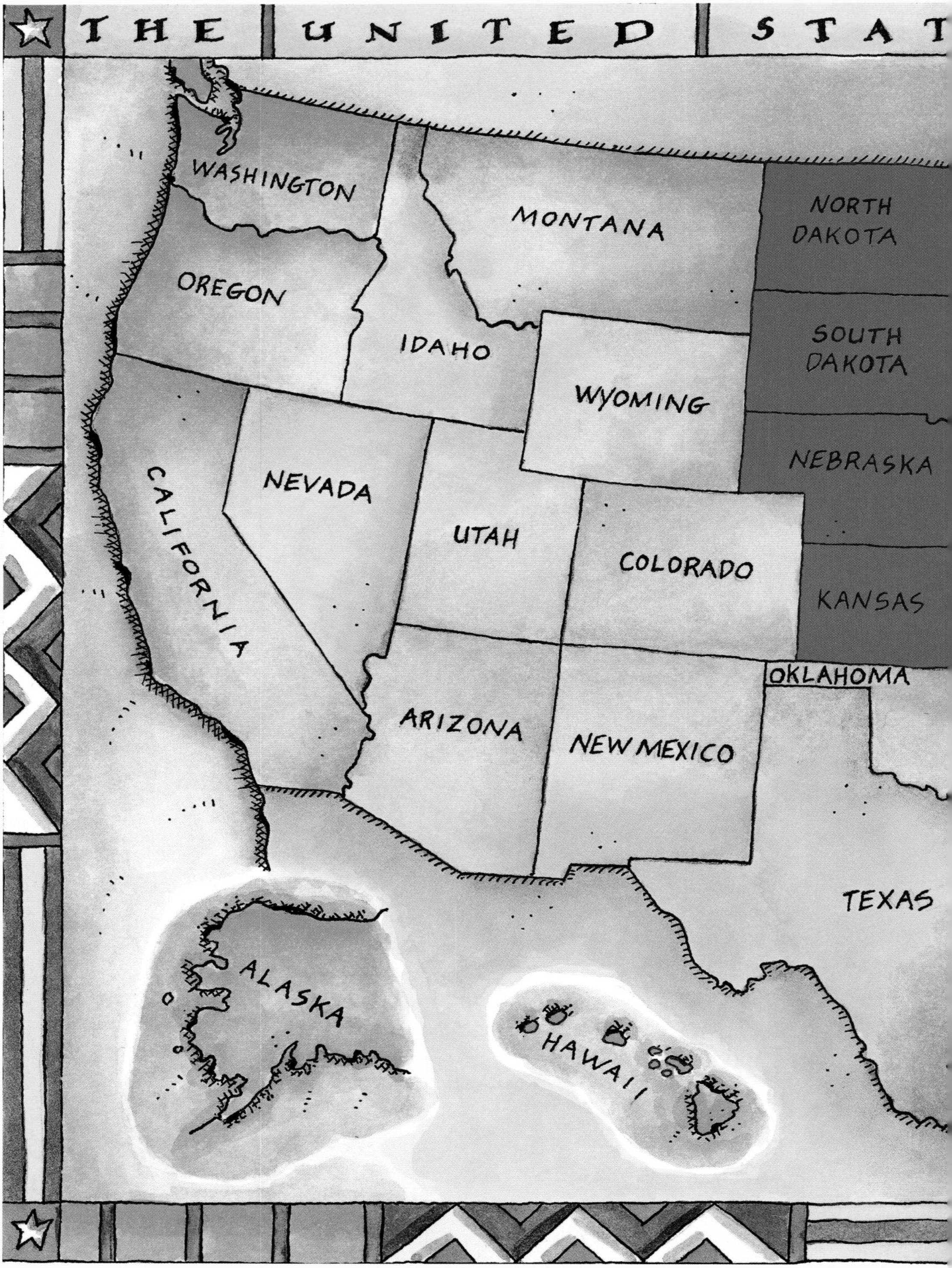

WASHINGTON

MONTANA

NORTH DAKOTA

OREGON

IDAHO

SOUTH DAKOTA

WYOMING

NEBRASKA

CALIFORNIA

NEVADA

UTAH

COLORADO

KANSAS

OKLAHOMA

ARIZONA

NEW MEXICO

TEXAS

ALASKA

HAWAII

MINNESOTA

WISCONSIN

MICHIGAN

IOWA

ILLINOIS

INDIANA

OHIO

MISSOURI

PENNSYLVANIA

NEW YORK

MASSACHUSETTS

RHODE ISLAND

CONNECTICUT

NEW JERSEY

DELAWARE

MARYLAND

WASHINGTON, D.C.

WEST VIRGINIA

KENTUCKY

VIRGINIA

NORTH CAROLINA

TENNESSEE

SOUTH CAROLINA

ARKANSAS

MISSISSIPPI

ALABAMA

GEORGIA

LOUISIANA

FLORIDA

NEW. HAMPSHIRE

VERMONT

MAINE

N

Midwestern States

NORTH DAKOTA

Origin of name	"Dakota" means friends in the Dakota Indian language.
Flag	The North Dakota state flag is dark blue. The first thirteen states are represented by thirteen stars. A bald eagle is in the center of the flag. The eagle holds arrows and an olive branch. The original thirteen states are represented by the red, white, and blue crest on the eagle's chest. In the eagle's talons is a scroll that reads *E Pluribus Unum* (one nation made up of many states). "North Dakota" is written on a red scroll beneath the eagle.
Capital	Bismarck
Nickname	Peace Garden State Flickertail State Roughrider State

Motto	"Liberty and Union, Now and Forever, One and Inseparable"
Size (in area)	19th largest
Bird	Western meadowlark
Fish	northern pike
Flower	wild prairie rose
Fossil	Teredo petrified wood
Fruit	chokecherry
Tree	American elm
Industry	agriculture, mineral production, tourism

NORTH DAKOTA MAP PILLOW

In 1988, the world's largest historical quilt was created to honor the one hundedth anniversary of North Dakota's statehood. The quilt is shaped like the state of North Dakota. Leona Tennyson of Antler, North Dakota, created the quilt. People from each of the fifty-three counties in North Dakota helped to stitch the quilt together. It covers more than 11,000 square feet, and weighs 800 pounds!

What you will need

* poster board
* markers
* scissors
* two large pieces of green felt, adhesive backed
* glitter pen
* puff paint
* cotton balls

What you will do

1. Draw the state of North Dakota on poster board with a marker. (See page 45 for pattern.) Cut it out (See A).

A)

B)

2. Trace the map onto two pieces of green felt. Cut out the two pieces (See B).

3. Write the name "North Dakota" across one of the pieces using a marker. Trace over the letters with a glitter pen. Let dry.

4. Pull backing off of the felt and match both pieces together on one side. Place cotton balls in the center. Finish closing the pillow. If you wish, deocrate the edge of the pillow with puff paint (See C). Let dry.

C)

MANDAN BEAR CLAW NECKLACE

During the winter of 1804, the Mandan Indians helped the explorers Meriwether Lewis and William Clark. The Mandan traded food for goods and taught the explorers about grizzly bears. The Mandan people used grizzly bear claws, fur, and beads to make necklaces. These necklaces were prized as important symbols of courage.

What you will need

* self-hardening clay
* scissors
* toothpick
* poster paint
* paintbrush
* glue wash (1/2 cup of white glue mixed with one cup of water)
* yarn
* 30 medium wooden beads

What you will do

1. Roll a piece of self-hardening clay into a 12-inch-long x 1/2-inch-wide piece (See A).

A)

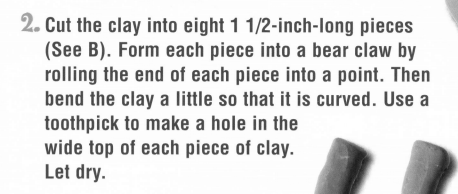

2. Cut the clay into eight 1 1/2-inch-long pieces (See B). Form each piece into a bear claw by rolling the end of each piece into a point. Then bend the clay a little so that it is curved. Use a toothpick to make a hole in the wide top of each piece of clay. Let dry.

3. Paint each piece of clay. Let dry. Coat each piece of clay with glue wash (See C). Let dry.

4. Cut a piece of string long enough to be a necklace. String the bear claws and wooden beads onto the yarn and knot the ends (See D).

B)

C)

D)

North Dakota **13**

SOUTH DAKOTA

Origin of name	"Dakota" means friends in the Dakota Indian language.
Flag	The South Dakota state flag is sky blue. The state seal is in the center of the flag and shows a farmer plowing his field, forests, mountains, a river, and a steamboat. The state's motto, "Under God the People Rule," also appears in the seal. A shining yellow sun surrounds the state seal. The words "South Dakota" and "The Mount Rushmore State" appear around the yellow sun.
Capital	Pierre

14

Nickname	**The Mount Rushmore State**
Motto	**"Under God the People Rule"**
Size (in area)	**17th largest**
Animal	**coyote**
Bird	**ring-necked pheasant**
Fish	**walleye**
Flower	**American pasqueflower**
Tree	**Black Hills spruce**
Industry	**lumber, livestock, manufacturing, agriculture, mining**

CORN MINI-MURAL

The Corn Palace is a very unusual building in Mitchell, South Dakota. Each year a festival is held there that includes dances, shows, and exhibits. The Corn Palace building is decorated each year with a new mural, or picture, made from ears of corn, grain, and grasses. The ears of corn are many different colors.

What you will need

* pencil
* poster board
* scissors
* white glue
* uncooked popcorn kernels
* green tissue paper
* yellow yarn (optional)
* puff paint

This tradition first began in 1892. South Dakota wanted to show the world that it was an excellent place for growing crops.

What you will do

1. Use a pencil to draw an oval on a piece of poster board (See A).

A)

B)

(See page 45 for the pattern.) Coat the inside of the oval with white glue. Place rows of popcorn kernels from left to right across the oval until it is filled (See B). Let dry.

2. Cut strips of green tissue paper, and glue around the ear of corn (See C). Let dry. If you wish, add yellow yarn for the corn's silk. Let dry.

3. Decorate the edge of the poster board with puff paint (See D). Let dry.

C)

D)

South Dakota   **17**

GALLOPING WILD HORSE

The Black Hills Wild Horse Sanctuary is near Hot Springs, South Dakota. The sanctuary covers 11,000 acres of land. More than five hundred wild horses live in safety there and are free to roam. Horses that have been abused are also adopted by the sanctuary and given a home.

What you will do

1. Draw a horse on poster board. (See page 46 for the patterns.) Cut out the pieces. Punch a hole in each piece where marked (See A).

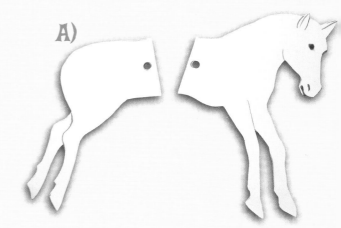

A)

2. Connect the two pieces of the horse with the brass paper fastener (See B).

3. Glue on yarn for the mane and the tail. Let dry. Glue craft sticks to the back of the horse, above the front and back legs (See C). Let dry. Paint the horse with poster paint (See D). Let dry.

B)

C)

D)

NEBRASKA

Origin of name	"Nebraska" comes from the Oto name for the Platte River, *nebrathka*, which means flat water.
Flag 	The Nebraska state flag is blue. The state seal is in the center of the flag and is gold and silver in color. A scroll at the top of the seal reads "Equality Before the Law," which is the state motto. In the center of the seal, a blacksmith is working. A log cabin, wheat, a steamboat, and mountains are behind him. There is also a train in the background, representing the transcontinental railroad. Around the seal are the words, "Great Seal of the State of Nebraska March 1st 1867."
Capital	Lincoln

Nickname	**The Cornhusker State**
Motto	**"Equality Before the Law"**
Size (in area)	**16th largest**
Bird	**western meadowlark**
Flower	**goldenrod**
Fossil	**mammoth**
Insect	**honeybee**
Tree	**cottonwood**
Industry	**food processing, agriculture (wheat, soybeans, cattle, corn, hogs), manufacture of transportation equipment, machinery, and metals**

RAIN FOREST ANIMALS

The Lied Jungle at the Omaha Zoo in Nebraska is the largest indoor rain forest in the world. It is 80 feet tall, and spreads across 1.5 acres. There are about ninety different species of animals in the Lied Jungle, including pygmy hippos, otters, spider monkeys, Goliath herons, clouded leopards, and Giant Indian fruit bats.

What you will need

* shoe box
* paintbrush
* blue and green poster paint
* index cards
* markers
* craft foam
* scissors
* construction paper
* white glue
* glitter pens

What you will do

1. Place the shoe box on its side. Paint the inside back, top, and two short sides of the shoe box blue. Paint the bottom long side of the shoe box green (See A). Let dry.

A)

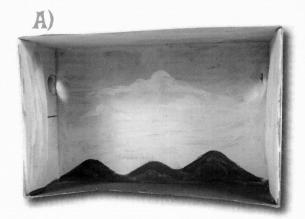

2. Draw a leopard, spider monkey, and hippo on index cards. (See page 46 for the patterns.) Cut out the animal shapes (See B). Trace the shapes onto craft foam with a marker. Cut out.

B)

3. Draw details on the animals with markers (See C). Set aside.

C)

4. Draw jungle plants and leaves on construction paper (See D). Cut out the shapes.

D)

5. Glue the animals to the inside bottom and back of the shoe box. Glue the leaves and the plants around the animals (See E). Let dry. Add details with markers and glitter pens if desired. Let dry.

E)

BUFFALO BILL'S HAT

"Buffalo Bill" Cody lived during the 1800s. He was a Pony Express rider, an Army scout, a buffalo hunter, a cowboy, and even a gold miner for awhile. When he was about twenty-six years old, Buffalo Bill became a showman. He traveled with Wild Bill Hickok and Annie Oakley, who were part of his Wild West show. Two of Buffalo Bill's homes are now at the Buffalo Bill Ranch State Historical Park in North Platte, Nebraska.

What you will need

* brown felt
* scissors
* small round plastic container
* white glue
* black marker
* poster board
* red felt
* glitter pen

What you will do

1. Cut brown felt to cover the outer sides and bottom of the round plastic container. Glue the felt to the container (See A). Let dry.

2. Trace the wide part of the round container onto the poster board with a marker. Draw an

A)

oval around the circle. The oval should be 4 inches wider and 5 inches longer than the circle. Cut out the large oval. Then cut out the inner circle (See B). You may also wish to use the pattern on page 45 depending on the size of your round container.

B)

C)

D)

3. Trace the inner and outer parts of the poster board circle on brown felt with a marker. Cut out the felt circle. Glue the felt to the poster board and let dry (See C).

4. Slide the circle opening over the small end of the container.

5. Cut a one-inch wide piece of red felt that is just long enough to go around the wide part of the container. Write the name "Buffalo Bill" in marker on the felt (See D).

6. Draw over the marker letters with a glitter pen. Glue the red felt to the hat and let dry (See E).

E)

IOWA

Origin of name	"Iowa" comes from the Sioux American Indian word meaning beautiful land.
Flag	The state flag of Iowa is blue, white, and red. In the center, a large American bald eagle holds a blue scroll. "Our Liberties We Prize And Our Rights We Will Maintain" is written on the scroll.
Capital	Des Moines
Nickname	The Hawkeye State

Motto	"Our Liberties We Prize and Our Rights We Will Maintain"
Size (in area)	26th largest
Bird	eastern goldfinch
Flower	wild prairie rose
Rock	geode
Tree	oak
Industry	agriculture (grain, soybeans, pork, corn)

DANGLING STRAWBERRY

In front of the town hall in Strawberry Point, Iowa, there is a 15-foot-tall giant strawberry! The town of Strawberry Point was named after a hill nearby where many wild strawberries grew.

What you will need

* terra cotta self-hardening clay
* sesame seeds (Ask permission first.)
* green pipe cleaner
* one foot of thin green ribbon

What you will do

1. Roll a piece of clay into an egg shape. Narrow the egg shape at one end to form a strawberry shape. Press sesame seeds into the clay. Bend the green pipe cleaner to form loops. Press the ends of the loops into the top of the strawberry. Let dry.

2. Thread the ribbon through the pipe cleaner loop and knot. Hang the strawberry.

GIANT SLOTH HOLIDAY MAGNET

The giant Ice Age sloth looked a little scary. This animal moved very slowly and it may have eaten grasses. Some of these huge animals stood ten feet tall and weighed as much as a small elephant. Rusty, a replica of a giant Ice Age sloth, stands at the University of Iowa's Museum of Natural History. At various times, Rusty has been seen wearing a Santa Claus hat, bunny ears, and even a Hawaiian grass skirt! Children in Iowa enjoy visiting the museum to see Rusty's latest costume.

What you will need

* poster board
* black marker
* scissors
* yellow or brown craft foam
* craft foam scraps
* self-adhesive magnet strip
* white glue

What you will do

1. Using a black marker, draw a giant sloth onto poster board (see page 44 for the pattern). Cut it out (See A). Trace the shape onto yellow or brown craft foam. Cut it out.

A)

2. Draw eyes and claws on the sloth shape with a marker (See B).

3. Stick a magnet onto the back of the sloth (See C).

4. Use small pieces of craft foam to make a funny hat for the sloth (See D). Glue the hat to the top of the sloth's head (See E). Let dry.

B)

C)

D)

E)

MISSOURI

Origin of name	"Missouri" comes from the Missouri American Indian word meaning town of the large canoes.
Flag	Missouri's state flag has red, white, and blue stripes, with the Missouri coat of arms in the center. Twenty-four stars show that Missouri is the twenty-fourth state. In the coat of arms on the right, the American bald eagle holds arrows and olive branches. Two bears on either side of the shield represent the bravery of Missouri's people. In a circle around the shield are the words "United We Stand, Divided We Fall." A gold scroll that is underneath the bears reads *Salus Populi Suorema Lex Esto.* The Roman numeral MDCCCXX, or 1820, is beneath the scroll. Missouri's struggles on the road to becoming a state are shown as a cloud over the large star. The helmet over the shield indicates that Missouri is a sovereign state.
Capital	Jefferson City

Nickname	The Show Me State
Motto	*Salus populi suprema lex esto* (This is a Latin phrase which means the welfare of the people shall be the supreme law.)
Size (in area)	21st largest
Amphibian	American bullfrog
Animal	Missouri mule
Bird	bluebird
Flower	white hawthorn blossom
Tree	flowering dogwood
Industry	service industries, tourism, travel, transportation equipment, manufacturing, lead mining, food processing, agriculture, livestock

PEACE SIGN COLLAGE

What you will need

* markers
* poster board
* scissors
* magazine clippings that depict the idea of peace
* white glue
* glitter pens (optional)
* clear tape
* yarn

Independence, Missouri, is home to the Children's Peace Pavilion. Here, children can learn about peace and how to be a peacemaker. The Pavilion has four ideas about peace: Peace for Me, Peace for Us, Peace for Everyone, and Peace for the Planet.

What you will do

1. Draw a peace symbol with a marker on a piece of poster board. (See page 46 for pattern.) Cut out the peace symbol (See A).

2. Cut out words and pictures that show the idea of peace (See B). These could be peace

A)

signs, doves, white flowers, the word "peace," the hand sign for peace, or a picture of something or someone that represents peace to you. Glue them to the peace symbol. Let dry.

3. Write the word "peace" on the peace sign in different places with markers. If you wish, decorate the peace symbol with glitter pens (See C). Let dry.

4. Tape a 8-inch piece of yarn to the back of the peace symbol for hanging.

FROG CLICKER

What you will need

* index card
* markers
* scissors
* plastic soda bottle cap
* thread
* toothpick
* white glue

The American bullfrog is Missouri's state amphibian and the biggest frog in the state. The American bullfrog makes a funny low sound to communicate with other frogs. Some people say the bullfrog sounds like it is saying "jug-o-rum."

What you will do

1. Draw a frog on the unlined side of an index card with markers. (See page 44 for the pattern.) Color in the frog as you wish with markers. Cut out the frog (See A). Set aside.

2. Wrap thread around the center of a plastic soda bottle cap thirty times (See B). Knot the thread.

A)

3. Push a toothpick through the center of the threads on the inside area of the bottle cap (See C). Push the toothpick far enough through the threads until you can turn the toothpick over completely. Repeat until there is tension on the toothpick so that it makes a clicking sound when it is pulled down slightly.

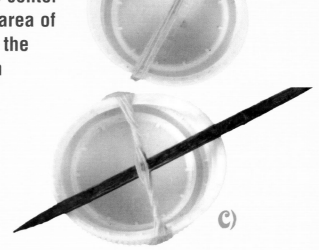

B)

C)

4. Glue the frog to the top of the bottle cap (See D). Let dry. Pick up the frog and push down on the toothpick to make it click.

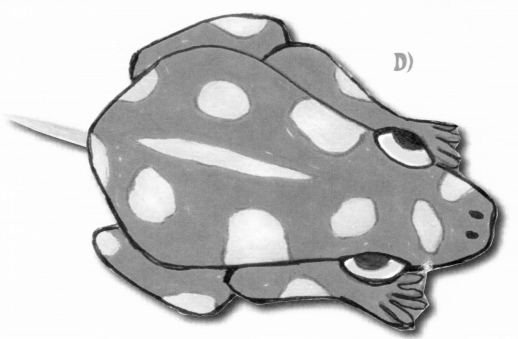

D)

KANSAS

Origin of name	"Kansas" comes from the Kansa or Kaw American Indians, which means people of the south wind.
Flag	The Kansas state flag is blue, with the state's name at the bottom of the flag in large gold letters. The state flower, the sunflower, is at the top of the flag, above the Kansas state seal. Covered wagons, American Indians hunting, a farmer plowing, a steamboat, and the rising sun are shown in the state seal. Thirty-four stars represent Kansas as the thirty-fourth state in the United States. The Kansas state motto appears in Latin, *Ad Astra Per Aspera*, at the top of the seal. This means "To the stars through difficulty."
Capital	Topeka
Nickname	The Sunflower State

Motto	***Ad astra per aspera*** **(This is a Latin phrase which means to the stars through difficulties.)**
Size (in area)	**15th largest**
Animal	**American buffalo**
Bird	**western meadowlark**
Flower	**wild sunflower**
Reptile	**ornate box turtle**
Tree	**cottonwood**
Industry	**agriculture (wheat, sorghum, alfalfa, oats, popcorn, rye), livestock**

STATE FLOWER MAGNET

What you will need

* craft sticks
* white glue
* poster board
* pencil
* scissors
* tiny black beads
* scraps of yellow fabric or craft foam
* self-adhesive magnet strips
* glitter pens (optional)

In Goodland, Kansas, there is a giant artist's easel that is 80 feet tall. It has a huge painting on it. The artwork is of sunflowers and it was painted by Cameron Cross. Sunflowers are an important industry in the Goodland area. The town is known as the "Sunflower Capital of the Sunflower State."

What you will do

1. Glue the ends of four craft sticks together to form a square (See A). Let dry.

2. Draw a square on a piece of poster board that is a little bigger than the opening of the craft stick square. Cut out the square.

A)

3. Make a circle of glue in the center of the poster board square. Sprinkle black beads in the glue. Let dry.

4. Cut out petal shapes from yellow fabric or craft foam. Glue the petals around the bead center of the flower (See B). Let dry.

5. Glue the poster board square to the craft sticks and let dry.

6. Stick the magnet strips to the back of the square (See C). If you wish, decorate the frame (See D).

B)

C)

D)

AMELIA'S FIRST AIRPLANE PATCH

The courageous American female pilot, Amelia Earhart, was born in Atchison, Kansas, in 1897. Her first airplane was a yellow plane that she called "the Canary." Amelia Earhart was the first woman to fly across the Atlantic Ocean alone without stopping. In 1937, Amelia Earhart began a trip with the hope of flying around the world. Her plane disappeared over the Pacific Ocean.

What you will need

* ✳ pencil
* ✳ poster board
* ✳ scissors
* ✳ self-adhesive felt
* ✳ yellow, red, and black puff paint

What you will do

1. Draw an airplane shape onto poster board. (See page 44 for the pattern.) Cut it out (See A).

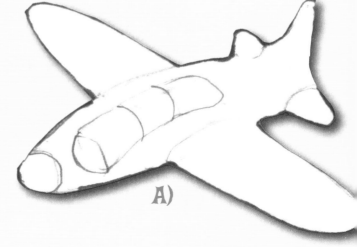

A)

2. Trace the airplane shape onto stiff felt. Cut it out (See B).

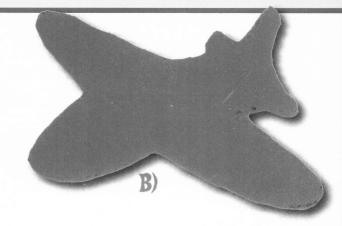
B)

3. Use the puff paint to add detail to the airplane shape (See C). Let dry.

4. Remove the backing and, with adult permission, place the patch on a notebook, a backpack, or a book cover.

C)

PATTERNS

Use tracing paper to copy the patterns on these pages. Ask an adult to help you cut and trace the shapes.

Amelia's First Airplane Patch

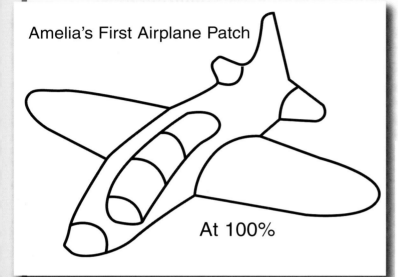

At 100%

Giant Sloth Holiday Magnet

Enlarge 200%

Frog Clicker

At 100%

44

North Dakota
Map Pillow

Enlarge 250%

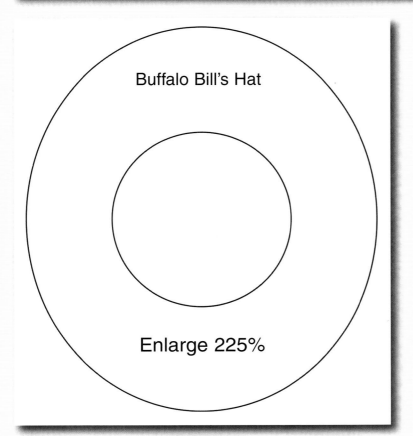

Buffalo Bill's Hat

Enlarge 225%

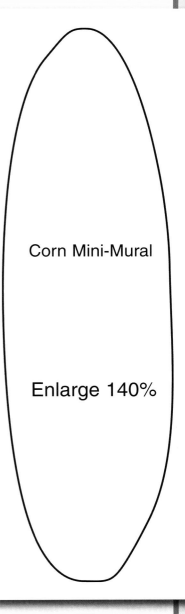

Corn Mini-Mural

Enlarge 140%

45

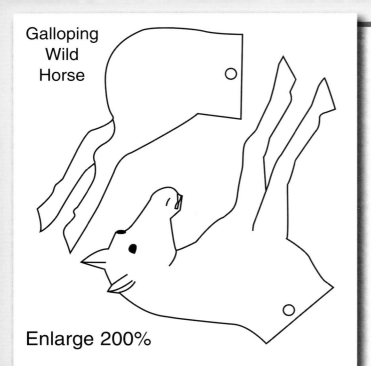

Galloping
Wild
Horse

Enlarge 200%

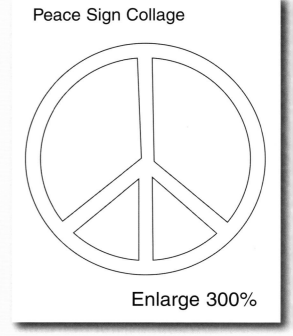

Peace Sign Collage

Enlarge 300%

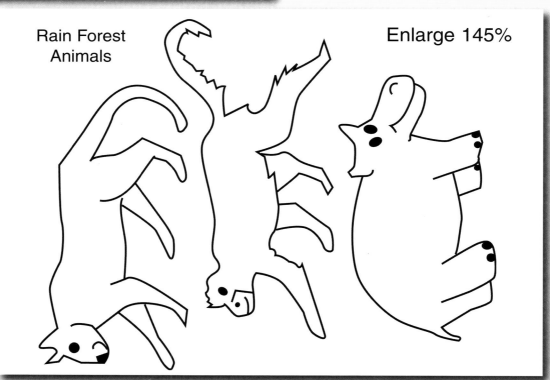

Rain Forest
Animals

Enlarge 145%

LEARN MORE

Books

Boekhoff, P.M. *Missouri*. Milwaukee, Wisc.: Gareth Stevens Pub., 2006.

Gibson, Karen Bush. *North Dakota: Facts and Symbols*. Mankato, Minn.: Capstone Press, 2003.

Heinrichs, Ann. *South Dakota*. Minneapolis, Minn.: Compass Point Books, 2004.

Morrice, Polly and Joyce Hart. *Iowa*. New York: Marshall Cavendish Benchmark, 2007.

Shepherd, Rajean Luebs. *C is for Cornhusker: A Nebraska Alphabet*. Chelsea, Mich.: Sleeping Bear Press, 2004.

Thomas, William David. *Kansas*. Milwaukee, Wisc.: Gareth Stevens Pub., 2006.

Internet Addresses

50states.com
    <http://www.50states.com/>

U.S. States
    <http://www.enchantedlearning.com/usa/states/>

INDEX